Indian Hunting

INDIAN
HUNTING

Written and Illustrated by
ROBERT HOFSINDE
(Gray-Wolf)

WILLIAM MORROW & COMPANY
New York, 1962

By the Same Author:

THE INDIAN AND THE BUFFALO

THE INDIAN AND HIS HORSE

INDIAN BEADWORK

INDIAN GAMES AND CRAFTS

INDIAN PICTURE WRITING

INDIAN SIGN LANGUAGE

THE INDIAN'S SECRET WORLD

Fourth Printing, March, 1967

Library of Congress Catalog Card Number 62-8273

To Larry Koller,
sportsman and big-game hunter.

Contents

Indian Hunting

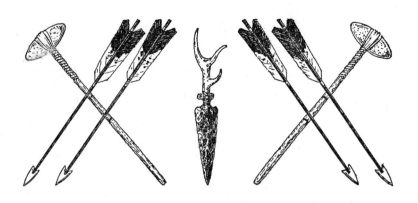

1

The Quest for Food

ONE of man's earliest struggles was his struggle for food. Whether his home was little more than the shelter of a rock or an abandoned cave, the need for food faced him day by day. We can only guess roughly at what early man ate, but the remains of animal bones give us some clue to his diet.

Scientists have established that man lived on this continent more than 20,000 years ago. He came from Asia, crossing over Bering Strait, either by dugout canoe or over a frozen land bridge, for it was during the ice age that he migrated here. This human being was a Mongoloid, and he quite possibly followed the game that had gone ahead of him.

One of these animals was the great, ancient bison. Weighing close to 2250 pounds, the shaggy animal was twenty-five per cent heavier than the bison, or buffalo, of today. This early giant arrived here more than fifteen million years ago, and with it came the mastodon, the ancestor of the elephant. Giant bears and camels also came, and some of these animals have been found, frozen and fully preserved, in the arctic tundra.

When we compare the size of man with the size of such animals, and then look at the stone-headed clubs and the short, dartlike spears with which early man hunted them, we wonder how he survived at all. His hunting was a hand-to-hand struggle, and many a hunter was killed by the animal he sought to kill.

As time passed, stone tools and weapons be-

SHORT SPEAR

ROCK, EARLIEST WEAPON

STONE HEAD, WOOD HANDLE.

STONE, TWISTED HIDE.

came stronger. At first man had encased a rock in a piece of skin, twisting the ends of the skin together to form a handhold. Now he added a wooden handle to the weapon, so he could use it more easily. He continued to search for safer ways to encounter wild game, and finally he discovered the bow. With a strong bow and a handful of arrows, man now had an even better chance for survival.

Man also began to study the things around him and watch the ways of the animals. He learned that, disguised in the skins of the wolf, he was able to stalk close to game. He also learned to come upon game against the wind.

Through the thousands of years that followed, man's brain developed more and more. He became as cunning as the fox, the wolf, and the raccoon. He observed the migratory habits of animals and birds. He discovered the regular game trails leading to water, and he learned to prepare for the lean months of winter by drying or smoking his surplus food, and thus preserving it.

Seasonal changes together with local conditions in various parts of the country developed different cultures among the people whom we today call the American Indian. Their hunting methods differed. Some hunted on foot, others by dugout or bark canoe, by snowshoes or dog sled, or, finally, by horseback.

Judged by our modern standards, the Indian was a primitive man, but, primitive or not, he became skilled in the ways of the forest. The earliest white people coming to these shores could not have survived in the wilderness without the help they got from the friendly Indian tribes they encountered.

The plains, the lakes, the mountains, and the forests abounded with game, and the Indian hunted these wild creatures for food alone. Now because we hunt for sport and because we have destroyed many natural food sources for animals, there are only a few places left where we can see wild life living as it did in the day of the Indian.

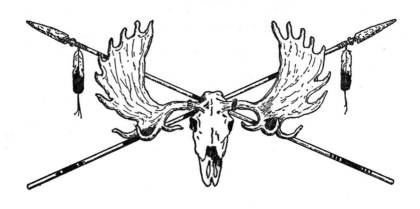

2
Hunting Large Game

THE Indians appear to have hunted deer more widely than any other animal. They hunted the white-tailed deer from coast to coast, and from Canada to Mexico.

The method they used most often was that of still-hunting. Once an Indian reached his hunting area, he rarely roamed the woods in search of game. Instead, he remained quietly in one place, letting the game come to him. Among the Ojibwa, the Winnebago, and the Menominee Indians of Michigan, Wisconsin, and Minnesota, men often hunted singly or in pairs.

A lone Ojibwa might take to a narrow trail leading to a clear, cool pool deep within the forest. Walking over dry pine needles and old leaves, his moccasined feet made scarcely more noise than the rustling sound caused by a scurrying field mouse. As he neared the end of his trail, his movements became even slower and he walked as silently as it is humanly possible to do. Upon reaching the pool, he seated himself on a nearby fallen log and wrapped his robe closely around himself. Across his knees he placed his bow with an arrow nocked on the bowstring.

As he sat there, motionless in the flickering shadows of the overhanging, leafy branches, he blended so fully into his surroundings that the birds, disturbed by his coming, were soon flitting about as before. The chipmunks again darted in and out among the rocks, and a gray squirrel emerged from behind a tree trunk to sit once again on a branch, flicking its bushy tail.

17

Into this tranquil setting walked a deer. Cautiously it sniffed the air without detecting the hunter. Unsuspecting it walked to the edge of the pool. Still on its guard, it carefully scanned the woods beyond the pool, but sensing no danger from there, it bent its head to drink.

Up until now, the hunter had not made a single move. Through half-closed eyes he barely followed the action of the deer. But as the deer drank, the hunter slowly, very slowly, raised his bow. Then he drew back the arrow to its flint point and let it fly.

Hit, the buck tensed for a moment, then fell dead.

Skinning out the deer, the hunter removed the heart and the liver, and took them back to the wigwam with him. From there he sent his wife and daughter back to the pool to bring back the hide, meat, and the bones.

The Indians preferred to still-hunt, for they were not topnotch archers and had to come quite close to the game to be sure of a hit. To overcome this drawback in their hunting, the Indian became

GRAY-WOLF.

thoroughly familiar from childhood on with the habits of the many animals he hunted for food. He gained knowledge of the game trails. He learned to read the tracks in the trails so that he could often tell from them how much time had elapsed since the animal had passed by. In fact, he learned to think much as the animals themselves might think.

When they did not still-hunt, two Indians might take the trail together to some clearing in the forest where they knew the deer would come to feed. At the edge of the woods by the clearing, they dropped to the ground. Slowly, on hands and knees, they then began to creep forward, taking advantage of sheltering rocks and brush.

From long observation they had learned that if the animals were feeding, it was safe to move ahead. However, they never for one moment took their eyes off the deer, and at the first flick of the animal's tail, the hunters flattened out. This flicking of the tail, they knew, was an indication that the deer would stop feeding, lift its head, and look around. As soon as the animals resumed feeding, the hunters again inched forward, stopping again and again when the deer moved, until at last they had come close enough to shoot accurately.

At other times Indian hunters attracted deer with artificial calls or smoke. They made a deer caller by carving out four cone-shaped pieces of wood. Each cone was tapered at one end so as to fit snugly into the hollowed-out wide end of the other. Into the second section from the mouthpiece they fitted a thin reed. It had just enough room to vibrate when the hunter called through the cones. To produce the proper sound, the Indian alternately cupped and opened his hand over the open end as he made the call. The resulting sound was very much like that of a fawn calling for its mother.

To attract deer with smoke, the Ojibwa used the dried and powdered roots from either the New England aster or the bearberry. After building a small fire, the hunter added the dried roots to it. If he had placed his smoke lure properly, the wind wafted the smoke toward the feeding deer. Attracted by the fragrance, the deer slowly moved into the range of the waiting and hidden hunters.

The Hopi Indians of the Southwest hunted the smaller Arizona white-tailed deer, which is rusty brown in summer and gray in winter, but in a manner quite different from that used by the northern woodland Indians. The men went out from the village in large numbers and formed a large, human circle around the feeding deer. Once the circle was completed, two of the men walked quietly in among the animals and slowly drove them toward the ring of hunters, who then shot them with bows and arrows.

The Zuñi tribes, able to obtain wood, built large fenced enclosures and then drove the deer into them. In some instances, a Pueblo hunter used an artificial deer caller made from a hollow gourd.

The tribes, such as the Ute, Paiute, Shoshoni, Bannock, Nez Percé, Flathead, and the Blackfeet Indians, who lived in or close to the Rocky Mountains hunted the mule deer. Although other hunters tried to come upon game so that the wind blew from the deer toward themselves, the hunters

GRAY·WOLF.

BEARBERRY.

NEW ENGLAND ASTER.

in the mountains often had to get above their game. Among the lofty peaks, especially in the morning, the air rises from the valley floor, and any animal above a human hunter would soon detect him. To be successful, the hunting party had to get well above the timber line and range downward.

At times the hunting party spent a day or so in a high camping spot before the actual hunting started. They did this to give any animal a chance to settle down again if it had come across their scent as they had climbed upward. As the hunting started, the party gradually worked its way down. When the deer came out on the open, sunny slopes to munch on the grass, the hunters came upon them.

In this type of country a strong bow and a close shot counted for much. If the animal was not killed outright, it might leap and fall down the steep mountainside, landing where no hunter could possibly retrieve it.

In the earlier days, only the best parts of the meat could be carried back to camp after such a hunt. When the Indians obtained horses, however, they packed all the meat back on them.

The Indians also hunted other large game. In the north country bordering on Canada, they hunted moose and caribou. The moose was valued for its meat as well as for its hide, and the Indians became experts in calling it from the deep woods with megaphones made from birch bark. Indians and white hunters still call moose this way today, and the reason why the moose comes to this call is explained around the evening fires of many tribes. The Penobscot Indians of Maine tell the following story.

Long ago the moose was a giant. He was so tall that he used to browse on the tops of the tallest trees in the forest, and no one dared to hunt him. He became very troublesome, especially when he walked right through a village, destroying everything in his path.

Finally a great and powerful old medicine man had enough of this trouble with him. After much singing and consulting with his medicine spirits,

25

he started for the deep woods. There he gathered up a large piece of birch bark and trimmed it with his stone knife. First he made it as long as his arm from elbow to finger tips. Then he rolled it into a cone, making the wide opening as large as the distance from the heel of his thumb to the tips of his fingers. The narrow end, which was to be the mouthpiece, he made two fingers wide.

When the megaphone was done, he placed it on his lips and made a long, drawn-out call with it. *Eeeeeeeeeeeee-ooooooooo-yuh!* he called.

Many Indians had followed him, but were hiding well back in the brush. At first they did not hear any answer to the medicine man's call. Then the medicine man called again, ending the call with a coughlike grunt. This time the Indians heard, far in the distance, an answering call, and the third time the medicine man called, the moose came charging through the forest with lowered antlers.

Many of the hidden Indians ran for the village as fast as they could, but the old man stood his ground. When the charging moose saw him, he stopped in a cloud of dust and pine needles. With his head still lowered he glared at the old man.

Knowing now that his medicine was powerful, the old man stepped up to the moose and placed both hands between the great antlers. Then he began to push. As he pushed, the moose began to shrink. Smaller and smaller he became, until at last, when the medicine man stopped pushing, the moose had become the size he is today.

Then the medicine man told the moose to go back into the forest, never to come out into the open again unless he was called.

This same tale, with variations, is told by many tribes, and when Indians make a moose caller, or megaphone, today, they still use the measurements given in this old legend of long ago.

When the Indian hunter called moose, he usually walked deep into the woods. There he placed the megaphone on his lips and called. Often he rotated his head, ending the call by pointing the open end of the megaphone toward the ground. He waited patiently between calls, for he knew that sooner or later the moose would come, mistaking the call for that of a rival in its domain.

When calling moose while hunting from a canoe, the northern Indians faced the forest. When at last the call was answered, the Indian dipped his megaphone into the water and scooped some of it up. Then he let the water pour back slowly with a splashing sound. To the oncoming bull moose this sounded as if a cow moose were lifting her wet head from the lily pads among which she so often was found browsing.

Indians also used one other method to call moose. They slashed away at the underbrush with a discarded moose antler. This was an imitation of two bull moose fighting each other during the mating season.

In winter, when the snow lay deep, the Indians hunted moose in a different way. Discarding their moose calls for snowshoes, the woodland Indians tracked down the large animals. As they tried to escape the hunters, they bogged down helplessly in the deep, heavy snow and soon fell prey to the Indians' arrows or spears.

The mating call of the moose is long and drawn-out, but the woodland caribou emits a grunting sound. Before the snow covered the woodlands the Indians also called the caribou by megaphone. However, the caribou hunter did not remain in one spot as he made the call. Instead he walked among the dry leaves and snapping branches and twigs on the ground. When the caribou heard this crackling and snapping, together with the grunting call, it thought that another of its kind was in the woods and came charging out.

There was danger connected with the hunting of both moose and caribou. The caribou stood 3½ to 4 feet high at the shoulder and weighed from 150 to 400 pounds. The moose stood from 5½ to 7½ feet at the shoulder and weighed between 600 and 1800 pounds.

During the mating season the bulls of both species were in an ugly mood, and if they were wounded, their disposition did not improve. Many an Indian hunter was killed or injured by a wounded bull. The moose, having a set of antlers that measures six feet across and weighs around eighty pounds, could toss a hunter for some distance or crush him against the ground with little effort.

Still another dangerous big-game animal that the Indian hunted was the bear. North of Lake Superior they were found in great numbers. Although it took great daring to come face to face with a bear, and especially with a grizzly, the Indians did hunt them, for they were of great importance to their people.

Bear hunting was often done with the help of dogs. A bear can travel fast, but it seldom outruns dogs, and in the end will climb a tree to escape them. Once the dogs got on the scent of a bear track, the hunter had little else to do but follow them until the bear was treed.

In the West and Northwest the Indians lay in wait close to a stream where the bear came to fish for salmon, and then they shot him from ambush.

From time to time a warrior set out on the trail alone to kill a grizzly. He did this to show how brave he was, and if he was successful he wore a necklace made from the claws of the grizzly bear forever after to prove his deed.

Bear meat is excellent, and several gallons of

oil, for which the Indian had many uses, can be rendered from the meat. The Indians anointed their hair with it, and in early summer they rubbed their bodies with it to keep off the swarms of black flies and mosquitoes. Bear fat is also a fine substitute for butter, and they used it for cooking. Even the poorest piece of meat can be made palatable with the aid of this oil.

The thick fur of the bear made a soft mattress for a springy willow bed, and with the mattress below him and still another bear robe as a cover, the Indian could sleep warmly on a cold winter night.

In the plains areas the Indians hunted the swiftest animal in the country—the pronghorn antelope. Fortunately for the Indian hunters, the pronghorn is a most inquisitive animal. Anything strange or different will hold its attention.

When the Indians hunted antelope, they took advantage of its curiosity. A few hunters sneaked up on a feeding herd, usually in the very early morning hours when the dim light made objects blend with the earth. Then, as the sun rose, one of the hunters slowly raised a slender pole from behind a sheltering rock. At the tip of this pole fluttered a couple of eagle feathers, and sometimes strips of soft buckskin.

Sooner or later one of the feeding pronghorns noticed the fluttering objects. For a long moment it stood staring at them. Then finally its curious nature made it go closer to investigate. When it walked away, it caught the attention of other pronghorns in the group, and they followed it. Soon a number of them came within shooting range of the Indians.

The hunters, as usual, had placed themselves so that the wind, or the early morning breeze, blew *from* the animals and not *toward* them. Once the antelopes were close enough, the well-hidden hunters shot them with their arrows.

The average pronghorn weighed between 80 and 140 pounds, and they were not hard to carry back to the village.

Buffalo hunting, on the other hand, was a much more difficult matter, especially in the days when the Plains Indians were pedestrians. Once a large herd of buffalo had been reported by the scouts, the hunters set out for them. The women broke camp and followed in the wake of the men. It was easier in those early days, when there were no horses, the tepees were smaller, and the personal belongings fewer, for the Indians to move their village to the buffalo hunters than to transport the meat to the village.

At first the Indians usually hunted buffalo by running them over a cliff. They built a crude V-shaped wedge of earth and stone, which in time became overgrown with grass. The narrow end of the V was placed at the edge of a steep cliff and left slightly open. The arms of the V extended well out across the plains.

To entice the buffaloes into this trap, one man, called the buffalo caller, walked toward the feeding herd. Over his head and shoulders he wore a buffalo head, horns, and fur, and a large part of the hide hung down over his back. Acting much like the feeding animals, he swayed from side to side.

Buffaloes are as curious as pronghorns, and before long some of them moved toward the

34

buffalo caller. As soon as this happened, he slowly started to walk back into the **V**. As more and more buffaloes joined the first few, the Indian began to trot, then run. The nearest buffaloes started to run too, and soon the rest followed.

When the buffalo caller had started out, other Indians followed him, hiding themselves behind mounds along the arms of the **V**. When the herd was running well within the **V**, these Indians began to jump up, yelling and flapping their robes in the air. The noise and commotion usually succeeded in stampeding the herd, and the onrushing animals forced those in the lead to plunge over the cliff. At the last moment the buffalo caller jumped behind one of the mounds to get out of the way of the herd. Most of the buffaloes were killed by the fall, but below the cliff other hunters had been stationed to shoot any animals still alive.

By the time the hunt was ended, the women had moved up. While some of them re-erected the village, others came to the cliff bottom to skin the buffaloes and to transport the meat and hides back to the tepees on dog-drawn travois.

During large tribal buffalo hunts the men took

all their directions from an appointed hunt chief, and no man was permitted to hunt buffalo alone. However, when a small band of Indians camped away from the main tribe, two or three men were permitted to kill buffalo for use among their own group.

In order to come within shooting distance of the feeding animals, the hunters disguised themselves under wolfskins. Normally, the buffalo was not afraid of a few wolves, especially when the cows did not have calves, and wolves, as well as coyotes, were often seen on the outer fringes of the buffalo herds. Crawling on hands and knees, the Indians were able to approach quite close, and if they aimed their arrows well, they could at times down two or three animals before the rest became alarmed and took flight.

Once the Indians of the plains obtained horses, the pattern for buffalo hunting changed entirely. Then they rode down on a buffalo herd and either forced them to mill around, so they could shoot them, or killed them in a straight chase. There were also large travois horses to haul the meat

36

away, so there now was no need to move the village except when the buffalo herds were reported to be several days' journey away.

3
Hunting Small Game

THROUGHOUT the country the Indians also hunted a large variety of small game.

In the north country they hunted the snowshoe rabbit in large numbers, either by snaring them or by shooting them with bow and arrows. This little rabbit, brown in summer and white in winter, has the odd habit of stopping short and sitting up when it hears a sharp whistle. If a hunter whistles at a group of four or five rabbits, they will stop and he may shoot one. When one rabbit is shot, the others will run. But if the hunter whistles again, as we do when calling a dog, the fleeing rabbits will at once stop and sit up, and he may still get the rest.

Among the Hopi Indians of the Southwest, rabbit hunts were the main source of fresh meat. At times they used traps, but to catch large quantities of rabbits they used nets.

One of these nets, woven from strong cotton cord or, in earlier days, from brush, was set up across a large stretch of desert. Several fires were built and green grass thrown upon them to produce a smudge, as this was thought to blind the rabbits. Then the hunters formed two large, curving wings and gradually moved toward each other, closing in until they made a complete circle. They drove all the rabbits they enclosed into the net and killed them with rabbit sticks.

The rabbit sticks resembled the Australian boomerangs in shape, although they were not quite as curved. Also, the Hopi rabbit stick did not return to the thrower if it missed its mark, although it did bounce. When it was thrown, the stick might hit one rabbit, bounce off, and hit several others.

Whenever the hunt was for meat to be used ceremonially, the Hopi hunters were accompanied by a medicine man, who, once they were in the field, made offerings to the spirits of the rabbits. Only men were allowed to be present.

If the hunt was for everyday food, however, the women and young girls often participated, although they did none of the actual hunting. The women, and especially the young, unmarried girls, watched closely. As soon as they saw a rabbit hit, they rushed over and picked it up. The man whose rabbit stick had made the hit then presented the rabbit to the girl. After the hunt, the girl cooked and brought to the hunter a well-prepared meal. This gesture was, among the Hopi Indians, a form of courtship.

Many of the Pueblo tribes made soft, warm fur robes from rabbitskins. They cut the skins into strips about one-half inch wide. Sometimes they overlapped the ends of these strips and tied them together with cord made from yucca cactus. Other times they twisted the ends of the fur strips together while the skins were still wet. If the strips were left to dry this way, they held together as strongly as if they had been sewed.

The Pueblo weavers set two poles, reaching well over a man's head, into the ground as far apart as the weaver wished the width of the blanket to be. She then tied a slender stick horizontally across the top of the uprights and another one between the poles close to the ground. She wrapped the long strands of fur strips around these sticks starting at the top, then down under the bottom, up and over, until the entire frame was covered like a screen. Then the weaver tied the strips together by weaving yucca cord across the fur strips from top to bottom. When she was finished, she pulled out the two horizontal bars, and the robe was ready for use.

The northern woodland people, the Ojibwa, Winnebago, and Menominee, also made similar robes. Instead of tying the strips together with cord, however, they wove across the vertical strips

41

of fur with still more rabbit-fur strips. The finished robe, done in this type of basket weave, looked as if it were made of many small squares. It was very beautiful.

Beaver was another animal the Indians hunted for its meat, its fur, and for the fat stored in its tail. Before the Indians had steel traps, they discovered many ways to catch the beaver. One old method, often used by the Blackfeet and other tribes living in or near the mountains, was to drain a beaver dam, actually leaving the beaver population high and dry.

Indians in the woodland and river areas found that beavers could be attracted toward the canoe if they tapped on the edge of the canoe frame with the shaft of their paddle or with a knife handle. The sound of the tapping carried under the water and brought the beaver close enough to be killed.

The meat from the beaver was used for food, and its soft, thick pelt, warm and durable, made fur hats and mittens for the Cree in Canada and other Indians in the northern forests and mountain regions. They lined moccasins, too, with this fur for winter use, or they added an edging, or cuff, to keep the wearer's ankles warm. The fat stored in the beaver's tail was rendered by boiling and used for softening ropes, rawhide thongs, and snares.

The muskrat was another small-game animal hunted by Indian tribes living near rivers. When it calls to its mate, this little animal makes a low, friendly squeak. To lure the muskrat close, the Indian reproduced this call by sucking the back of his hand and making a sound much like that of a loud kiss.

Much of the smaller game the Indians hunted, such as rabbits, coyotes, and foxes, was caught in traps or deadfalls, which they constructed with great care.

The coyote trap made by the southwest Indian was the largest of all. First he dug a two-foot square into the earth. Within this square he placed a flat rock of nearly the same size. Along two parallel sides of this rock he placed two flat stones so that they stood on edge. He placed a third flat stone at an angle to the rock and held it up with a stick. He cut a notch into this stick and placed the bait in it. Finally he placed the stick on a small, round stone. When the coyote walked into the trap and pulled at the bait, the stick slipped off the round stone and the flat stone dropped down on the animal.

These Indians trapped prairie dogs in a similar way, but the trap was smaller and the bottom rock was placed on the surface of the ground instead of in a hole. Coyote bait was a piece of meat, but prairie-dog bait consisted of seeds.

Perhaps the simplest trap was the one used for rabbits, which used only a single kernel of corn as bait. The Indians placed a flat stone on the ground and set up another flat stone at an angle against it. They held the second stone in place with a stick set upright under it. This stick was placed on top of the corn kernel. When the rabbit tried to pull out the kernel, it sprang the trap.

The woodland Indians, such as the Iroquois, Ojibwa, Winnebago, Menominee, Fox, Potawatomi, and many others, also used similar traps. Often, however, they made them with heavy logs in place of rocks and stones.

FIGURE 4 TRAP

COYOTE TRAP

←BAIT

CORN.

RABBIT TRAP

The largest of these traps is called a figure four because of the way it was built. It was set between two trees, which served as a frame, and it was made from three straight saplings. One of these stood upright in the ground. Another, set horizontally, was notched into the middle of the upright, and the third was set at an angle between the upright and horizontal pieces. One end of the third sapling rested on top of the upright, and the lower end fitted into a notch in the horizontal bar. A notch at the other end of the horizontal bar held the bait.

To this framework a heavy log was then added. Carefully balanced, one end of the log rested on the ground, while the rest of the log was placed on top of the slanting pole of the figure four.

When an animal upset the balance of the delicately constructed trap to get at the bait, the log fell on top of it.

Snares were also set to catch rabbits and birds along the animal runs. Such runs were used almost daily by the animals to reach the streams or their favorite feeding grounds. The Indians usually found a bird or rabbit in their snares at the end of the day.

To set such a snare, an Indian bent down a young sapling across the trail, or run, and set it into a notch cut into another sapling. He made a loop from a thin strand of sinew and suspended it from the tip of the bent sapling so that it rested partly on the ground.

A rabbit following its usual run would walk into the loop, releasing the bent sapling from the notch. Then the bent sapling sprang upright with the rabbit caught in the loop.

Indians made bird snares from a single strand of human hair. They looped one end and fastened the other end to a stake set into the ground. The loop rested flat on the ground, and sooner or later the feeding bird would hop into the loop, pulling it and tightening it around its feet.

If the Indians wanted to trap larger animals, they dug a deep pit in the ground, often using the shoulder blade from a large deer as a digging tool. They covered the pit with dry branches and then covered the branches with grass and dry leaves. Any unsuspecting animal walking across such a spot broke the branches and fell to the bottom of the pit.

When the Indians later came back to the pit and found it occupied, they killed the animal with spears or arrows. After they removed the game, they usually covered the pit again to trap yet another meat supply.

Indian hunters also searched for crows, wild turkeys, snipe and killdeer, wild geese and ducks on their daily rounds. One bird, the spruce grouse, was very easy to catch. It was commonly known as the fool hen and came by that rather uncomplimentary name because it acts like a fool and can, actually, be caught with one's bare hands.

When an Indian discovered where some of these birds made their nightly roost, he arrived ahead of the birds and hid in the bushes nearby. The birds, as they came in to rest for the night, preferred to roost on the lower branches of a tree, and once they were asleep, the hunter could slip up to them silently.

Usually the hunter carried a stick with a short

SPRUCE GROUSE.

G.W.

buckskin noose at its upper end. The noose was tied in a slipknot, and as he slipped it over the head of the nearest bird on the lowest branch and pulled it to him, the noose tightened. With one quick motion he pulled the bird from the roost without disturbing any of the others.

Working his way from bird to bird and from branch to branch, the hunter could clear the entire roost. In some instances these birds have been known to be snared, one after the other, while still wide-awake.

The ruffed grouse was another bird that could be taken in the same way.

Indians made wild ducks and geese land close to shore by using decoys. Some of these decoys were very simple and made on the spot. They were nothing more than a large ball of mud or clay, roughly shaped in the form of a bird. The decoy maker tied a few short feathers to a stick and set it into one end of the clay ball to serve as neck and head. Several such decoys set up along the shore often fooled the birds and got them to land on the water nearby.

Some hunters, planning a little ahead, saved the heads from ducks taken on an earlier hunt. They then impaled them on the sticks in place of the feathers. As these heads could be placed so that some looked ahead, some backward, and others bent down as if feeding, the result was more lifelike.

Like some duck hunters today, many Indians had a supply of well-made decoys for permanent use, and they set them out upon the water when the birds migrated in spring and fall.

Sitting by his lodge fire during the long winter evenings, the Indian made these decoys from rushes and cattails. After he cut the rushes, he carefully dried them in a shady spot. Then, when they were ready for use, he bent and folded them and tied them together, layer upon layer, forming very lifelike bird forms. Sticks tied together in a rough cross were set in at the head end and wrapped with rushes to make the neck and the beak.

The Indian had carefully skinned his catch of water birds from former hunts and kept the skins

51

soft by rubbing the inner surface with animal fat. After he completed his reed forms, he carefully pulled a skin over each one, making the decoys look very natural. These decoys of dried, hollowed reeds also had another advantage over those made from clay, for they were more bouyant.

When such a natural-looking group was set out, the migrating ducks and geese readily landed in the coves. From a well-constructed blind on shore, the Indian shot at the wild birds with his bow and arrows and brought home a good supply of them for his winter store of food.

The Indians hunted eagles too, especially for their feathers. They were too high flying, though, to be reached with bow and arrows, and they usually had to be caught by hand. To do this, the Indian dug a deep pit at the top of some high butte. Then he covered the pit with brush. On top of the brush he placed his bait, which usually was a live rabbit, tied so that it could move about freely, but unable to run away. The hunter then stationed himself within the pit, waiting for the eagle to see the bait and to swoop down upon it.

CLAY.

RUSH DECOY

CLAY WITH DUCK HEAD.

WITH DUCK-SKIN COVER.

When at last an eagle appeared, it circled overhead for a while before coming in. Finally it landed, and the Indian reached up through the pit cover and grasped the eagle by the feet. Dragging an eagle down into such a pit was rough hunting, and the eagle did not stand for such treatment without putting up a fight. The Indian might have the eagle by its feet, but the bird could, and did, use its sharp beak. Once the eagle had been brought into the pit, the Indian killed it by stepping between its wings and breaking its back.

In this way the Indians of the plains got the eagle feathers for their war bonnets. Not only did the warrior have to earn the right to wear such a bonnet on the war trail, he had to fight in order to obtain the feathers.

4

Hunting from Canoes

THROUGHOUT the woodland areas, wherever birch bark was found, the Indians used the canoe as a means of travel. In fact, much of the early exploring of this country was done by canoe. Most of these Indians also used the canoe for hunting and fishing expeditions.

Although various tribes used slightly different designs to build birch-bark canoes, especially for the stern and bow, their main shape was much the same. They had a broad beam and a shallow draft, making it possible to paddle them across very low waters. Possibly the best known shape was that used by the Ojibwa Indians. It is this canoe, with a lower stern and bow, that is the model for canoes made today.

Night hunting from a canoe was not unusual, and on such trips the Indians often jack-lighted for deer. This method of hunting is forbidden by conservation laws today, but, of course, the Indians had no such laws then.

The Ojibwa Indians fitted their canoes with two long, slender poles. They fastened them under the forward spreader, so that they rested on the gunwales of the canoe and extended well out in front. Between the protruding ends they suspended a birch-bark box filled with sand into which they stuck a dry, pitch-filled pine knot. They also fitted across the poles, closer to the canoe, a broad piece of birch bark, which served as a shield for the hunters' eyes once the torch was lit.

A typical jack-lighting trip started at sunset. Leaving the village, the Indians paddled across

the lake toward the mouth of the river that emptied into it. By the time they crossed, darkness had set in, and they lighted the torch. They paddled into the river slowly and silently, for on a still night any sound will carry across water. Even the dripping water from a lifted paddle will make a loud sound.

Because of this an Indian never lifted his paddle above the surface. When he completed the backward stroke, he twisted his wrist and turned the paddle blade, cutting it through the water, so that he could make the return stroke in the water instead of in the air. With another twist of the wrist, he was again ready to stroke with his paddle, and in this way he was able to make his canoe glide ahead as silently as a night owl on the wing.

Once the hunters entered the river, the overhanging tree branches made the night even darker. In fact, everything outside the radius of the torchlight appeared coal-black. Then suddenly the blackness was pierced by two glowing, golden spots as the firelight caught and reflected in the eyes of a deer standing at the water's edge, where it had come to drink. The stern paddler held the canoe still and steady with his paddle, while slowly the hunter in the bow rose to a kneeling position.

In the tenseness of the moment the sounds of the night insects were greatly magnified. Then came the sharp twang of the bowstring as an arrow was released. This was followed by a splashing of water, a crashing in the underbrush, and a thud as the deer fell to the ground.

Paddling to shore, the men carefully lifted the deer into the canoe, watching closely to prevent hoofs and antlers from damaging the frail craft. Then they stepped into the canoe and pushed off from shore. As there now was little need for silence, both hunters gripped their paddles, and with quick, even strokes headed for the village.

We often think of the country around the Great Lakes as canoe country, and indeed it was. The Ojibwa, Chippewa, Menominee, and Winnebago Indians were especially known for their canoe travels. However, many other tribes, from the forest Potawatomi in Wisconsin to the Penobscot in Maine to the Seminole in Florida, used canoes, and in some instances dugouts, for their water travels.

Looking at the eastern half of the United States as it is today, it is perhaps hard to visualize that it once was covered with forest and that the easiest way to travel and hunt was by boat on the large rivers. Hunting from a canoe during spring, summer, and fall, however, was an almost daily task of these forest tribes, and not all their hunting was done by torchlight.

In the North the Indians sometimes hunted moose by driving it into a lake. The hunters then paddled up alongside it and killed it with spears. Such hunting was very dangerous, as the moose could at any moment turn around and, with a toss of its great antlers or a crash of its body, rip the canoe apart.

In the Far North caribou were hunted in the same way, and sometimes an Indian hunter made a deer swim a stream, so that he could then spear it.

In the southeastern part of the country the rather shallow dugout canoe used by the Seminoles was made from an old, well-seasoned cypress log. Although they had no level or measuring sticks, they made the craft so perfectly and with such stability that they sailed some as far as Cuba and the Bahamas. The prow was pointed and raised, the stern rounded, and the canoe was poled rather than paddled. In the swamplands where it was used, such as the Florida Everglades, the Indians did most of their hunting for birds, fish, wild turkey, and the smaller Florida deer from these boats.

The white birch used to make canoes was found all through the northern part of the country, from Long Island westward to the Rockies, and from Nebraska to Newfoundland, the Mackenzie River basin, and Alaska. In some areas the trees grew to a very large size, and a single piece of bark, stripped from such a giant, was enough to cover a canoe frame.

Yet in some parts of this country as, for example, New York State, the white birch did not grow large enough to use for canoe making. Although we often see the Iroquois Indians from this area depicted in birch-bark canoes, they originally made and used dugouts. Any large bark canoes they owned were made by tribes farther north with whom they traded.

The Ojibwa Indians made so much use of birch bark that they have been called the Birch-bark Indians. They learned that the bark forms on the trees in layers and that it has different thicknesses. The largest trees had from six to nine layers of bark. When removed in early spring, this bark was strong enough for canoe building. The layers could also be peeled apart into strips, thin as tissue, that were still strong enough to be used as wrappings for bundles.

In the gathering of bark, as in his hunting, the Indian was a true conservationist. He removed the bark so he did not injure the inner layer where the sap flowed. By so working, he did not kill the tree, and in time new layers of bark formed.

Whenever a birch was large enough to produce a single piece of bark for a canoe cover, the Indian first cut a circle around the tree trunk near the base. Sixteen to eighteen feet above this he cut another circle, and from the top circle to the bottom circle he cut a straight, vertical line. He then carefully removed the bark in one piece, rolled it up, and brought it back to camp, where he stored it in a shaded spot until ready for use.

Straight-grained wood, usually white cedar, was used for the framework of the canoe. The Indian carefully cut, split, and shaved it down to the proper size for ribs, thwarts or spreaders, gunwales, and keels. He then soaked these strips in a nearby stream or lake for several days, making them even more pliable.

Having no yardsticks, the Indians used body measurements in his building. The correct depth amidships of a canoe, for example, was the distance between a man's thumb and elbow. The proper distance between ribs in a canoe was the span of a man's hand from thumb to little finger.

Once the frame was ready, the builder placed the bark strip on the ground and held it in place with stones laid in a row along its center. Over this he placed a roughly made keel, shaped to the size of the canoe. He rolled the bark toward the stones on both sides and drove stakes into the ground along the two rolls.

After the builder placed a few ribs at random,

he fitted the gunwales. As the work progressed, he sewed the bark to the framework with fine strands of spruce root, tamarack, or jackpine. He made these strands more pliable by first boiling them in a broth made from fish.

As the work further progressed, he pulled the stakes gradually together in opposite pairs with spruce root, to hold the bark in place. When the canoe was covered and all the ribs had been inserted, the Indians turned it over, and one of the women crawled under it. If any cracks had developed in the bark, she could see daylight through them and she indicated where they were. Another woman, working from outside, then patched the spots with pine pitch. If the covering had been made from several pieces of birch bark, the places where the bark was overlapped were covered with pitch. The Indians often heated the pitch and mixed it with charcoal so that these patchings would make a more attractive design.

Canoes were made in various sizes, depending upon the use to which they were put. Small river canoes, which were paddled by two people and carried a small load or one extra person, ran about

sixteen feet in length. Others, such as those used by the French *voyageurs* and the *Boisbrûlé*, or burnt wood, as the French-Canadian half-breeds were called because of their dark skins, measured from thirty-five to forty feet.

With all the care and fine craftsmanship that went into the making of a canoe, it lasted only a little more than one year if it were used for long trips or for carrying large loads. Thereafter, it was kept by the village and used for short fishing trips, nearby visits, and for the children's use as they learned the fine art of handling the light watercraft.

The canoe paddle used by the Ojibwa was very simple. They usually made it from cedar, and it measured four feet in length, of which about one half was the blade. The blade itself measured from four to six inches at the widest part.

When he paddled, the Indian sat low in his canoe, kneeling and resting on his heels. On long trips he might use a kneeling pad. This low position is much safer than sitting on a high cane seat as the white man does.

Crossing a large body of water on a hot summer day, the Indians often used their paddles to obtain a drink. Swinging the blade up and placing the edge of it to his lips, he drank as the water ran off the blade.

5

Whales, Seals, and Salmon

THE climate, vegetation, and the abundant marine life of the Pacific Northwest made an ideal land for the Indians living in that region. They hunted seals, otters, and whales with harpoons, but only the Nootka were whale hunters.

The whaling canoes, built with special care, were about thirty feet long. They were hollowed out from the trunks of giant cedars, and were carved and highly painted with designs of whales, bears, and ravens.

Their harpoons had detachable heads with broad points. The points were made from either shell or stone and were lashed to the heads. Long lines of twisted cedar bark or whale sinew ran from the heads to floats of inflated sealskin. These floats served as drags once the whale had been harpooned, and they marked the whale's position when the lines were free of the canoes. They also prevented the whale from sinking after it had been killed.

The hunters carried spears and long-bladed knives as well. With this primitive equipment whale hunting was, to say the least, a dangerous experience, for the canoe had to come within a scant three feet of the whale in order to make a perfect throw of the harpoon possible.

When a whale hunt was called, a Nootka village sent out from three to ten large, seagoing canoes. The larger the fleet, the sooner the whale could be hunted down and harpooned.

The man leading such a whale hunt had usually inherited this job. Before each hunt he was required to go through special ceremonies to please his helping spirit. The prayer grounds, hidden in the forest, contained a number of carved wooden figures, representing whales. These shrines also contained the skulls of former whale chiefs. To show the spirits that he had fortitude, the chief's clothing on these trips to the prayer grounds was made from thorny wild rosebushes or from stinging nettles. The Indians had great respect for the giant whales, and they performed these ceremonies because they did not think that the powerful whale could be taken by human efforts alone.

Hunting and harpooning a whale was not always a matter of coming alongside it and killing it. There were times when a whale, after being harpooned, would tow a single canoe around the ocean for three or four days before it became tired enough to be lanced and killed. The Nootka thrust their harpoons as close to the whale's head as possible. This made the whale easier to handle, and it also kept the canoe a fairly safe distance from the whale's powerful tail. The lashing of this tail could, and at times did, upset a canoe.

A canoe carried a crew of eight men, each of whom had his own special task to perform. Most of these men were brave, but some were even more daring than the rest.

Usually the Nootka killed the whale with spears. However, a man gained great respect and admiration from his fellow tribesmen by leaping to the back of the harpooned whale and thrusting his long knife into it. Then, holding on to the handle of the knife, he stayed with the whale as it submerged. If he was able to remain with the whale until it surfaced again, he was thereafter known by the respected and honored name Stepping on a Whale.

There were other dangers involved in the whale hunts too. The grain of the wood from which the canoe was made ran lengthwise, and at times, when the seas ran high and the canoes were far from shore, a great wave would hit the canoe and split it like kindling from stem to stern.

71

WHALE LANCE

HARPOON HEAD

KNIFE

G.W.

Crew, tools, weapons, and boxes then went overboard. If no other whaling canoe was close by, few if any of the men made it back to shore, especially if they were several hundred miles out to sea.

At times a harpooned whale got away from the hunters and then died from its wounds later. Such whale carcasses eventually washed back to shore. If one landed on a shore where a tribe that did not hunt whales lived, these people were indeed happy to make use of it, and wasted nothing. They ate flesh and skin, made intestines into oil containers, used sinew for making rope and lines, and ate the blubber or turned it into oil. The man who discovered the whale was given the choicest pieces from it, and the rest was divided among the people according to their ranks and family standings.

The Northwest Coast Indians also hunted seals with harpoons, but they used smaller boats or dugouts for them. The harpoon they used usually had two points instead of one. The floats attached to the seal harpoon were made from bladders instead of sealskin.

The seal hunter also carried a spear and a highly carved wooden club with a round head. The seal, when hit, dived. If the harpoon held, the floats kept it from escaping. As soon as the seal was pulled out of the sea again, the Indian tapped it over the head with his carved club.

It is said that if a seal is killed while not held by a harpoon, it will at once sink under the surface and, unlike other bodies, it will not come to the surface again.

Living this close to the sea, it is not surprising that much of the food these Indians ate came from the ocean and rivers. Of all this sea food, three fourths was salmon, and the rest included halibut, cod, and candlefish.

When the salmon ran, the Indians harvested them as a farmer harvests his crops in the fall. They wedged fishing platforms into crevasses in the rocks above the river falls. First they set cedar poles so that they extended well out over the churning falls and river below. Then they built platforms, also from cedar poles, and rested them across this precarious framework. Its weight bent the platform steeply downward.

Close to the edge of such platforms, the men took their stand. With large nets tied to open hoops lashed on the ends of long, slender fishing poles, they dipped the salmon up as they came up the falls to spawn in the shallow pools far above.

Where the cliffs were sheer and the drop to the water great, the Indians figured out other methods to catch salmon. They built a ladderlike scaffold by lashing together long, slender poles, thicker than a man's arm, and spreading them apart with crossbars. Easing the scaffold over the cliffs, they somehow managed to set it up vertically, resting the bottom in the stream. Then they climbed down it, aided by ropes, dropping from one crossbar to the next. These bars were often spaced twelve to twenty feet apart. Standing just above the water and using a double-pointed, long-handled spear, the fisherman harpooned the salmon as they made their struggling way upstream.

In other places they set nets and basketlike fish traps to obtain salmon in season.

At the close of each day the men hauled the catch home to the village. Here the women split and cleaned the large fish. Much of the catch was dried by hanging it on racks in the sun and air. Later it was stored away for winter food. They pounded some of the dried fish to a pulp and stored it in waterproof casings of seal bladder.

When the salmon run ended the time for feasting had arrived. The women split, cleaned, and spread open the thick salmon flesh, and inserted the meat between two green cedar sticks. They set the sticks vertically into the ground around a large bed of hot coals and tied the upper ends together. They turned the salmon steaks from time to time until they were all well done, and the entire village stood by impatiently, waiting for the delicious feast to begin.

The dugout canoes, large and small, used by these Indians for whale hunting, sealing, fishing, or for setting out their fish traps, were made from cedar trees. Usually they selected a well-seasoned, fallen tree. After they removed all the dead limbs, they skidded the trunk down to the beach.

To make the large, seagoing canoes, they first burned out as much of the inside as possible, and then chopped the charred sections away with stone adzes. Once they hollowed the log to its proper thickness, they filled the interior with water. Then they threw rocks, heated in large fires, into it. At the beginning this work was dangerous, for as the heated rocks struck the water, they often exploded and stone chips flew in all directions. As the water became warmer, the stones stopped exploding and finally caused the water to boil. This softened the wood so that the builders could insert spreaders between the sides and make the canoe wider. They also bent the gunwales, so the waves would not wash inboard when the sea was rough.

The Indians then carved the high prow and stern from other cedar logs and fitted them in place with wooden pegs. They were such fine craftsmen that once the extra pieces were fitted, the seams were waterproof without covering them with pitch or spruce gum. The builders placed figureheads, in the shape of a bear, an eagle, or a raven, in the prow, not on the outside, as on our old sailing ships, but inboard. The stem and stern,

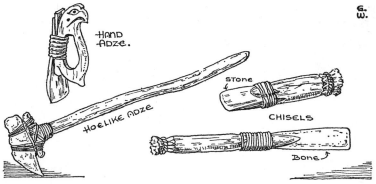

HAND ADZE.

HOELIKE ADZE

STONE

CHISELS

Bone

and at times the entire canoe, were decorated with painted designs in red, black, blue-green, and yellow. These designs most often depicted the killer whale.

In the early days the Indians propelled these large canoes with paddles, but after they came into contact with white sailors, they began to use a sail made from woven nettles.

Smaller canoes for travel on the rivers or in the inlets were built on the same lines, but usually they were not decorated.

So close to the sea were these people that when they died their last resting place was a canoe set on a high scaffold.

6
Preparing for the Hunt

TODAY when a white man prepares for a big-game hunt, he checks his gear and he makes reservations with an outfitter. The outfitter provides him with a base camp, a trail camp, food, pack horses, and guides.

The Indian, too, made preparations, but in a much different manner. He checked his weapons to see if he had enough arrows and a strong point on his spear, and he packed some pemmican. Then he danced.

The dances were animal dances and depended upon the type of game he planned to hunt. Each one was designed and performed to appease the spirits of the hunted animal. There were buffalo dances and deer dances, eagle dances and bear dances, to name a few, and they all had their own special song or collection of songs.

These dances were performed when the Indians prepared to go on a large tribal hunt. On the plains they danced the buffalo dance in imitation of the buffalo, hoping to bring this shaggy animal in great numbers. Deer and antelope dances were danced for the same purpose, and in the far northern sections of the country the caribou dance was performed.

The many tribes that hunted the bear, including the Northwest Coast tribes, did a bear dance in which the dancers carried artificial bear claws, held between the fingers. These dances included a great deal of stomping and grunting.

During October, the Falling Leaf Moon, as the Ojibwa Indians called it, came the time to prepare for the hunting of deer and other large game.

BUFFALO ·

DEER ·

EAGLE ·

ANIMAL DANCES

WOLF ·

G. W.

Winter was close by in the north country, and the evergreens stood darkly outlined against the flaming colors of the leaf-bearing trees. Within the birch wigwams fires were burning, and many of the lodges were filled with smoke as the hunters heaped sweet fern on the coals. Just as their ancestors had done in the past, so now the hunters stood in the enveloping smoke and let the sweet fragrance permeate their buckskin garments, removing all traces of human odors. Over the rafters hung their soft-tanned deerskin robes, which also needed to be smoked. When the smoking was completed, the men gathered up their weapons, food, and robes, and started on the hunting trail.

Nearly all the Indians carried with them some hunting charm. They believed it would assure them of a successful hunt, and they also believed that it had to be treated with respect. Such hunting charms were described in a dream. A dream person appeared and instructed the dreamer about the object and how to care for it, the songs to sing, and other rituals to perform.

A bear, for example, might come to a warrior

in a dream and tell him that from now on the bear people would be his brothers. Then, upon waking, the Indian went out in search of a bear. He killed it, and from its claws made himself a necklace. This necklace then became his hunting medicine. Before starting out on the hunting trail, he performed the proper rituals over the necklace, always down to the very last detail the dream bear had told him.

After slaying the bear, the Indian placed a piece of meat or pemmican in its mouth to appease its spirit, and he told the bear that he was sorry to have made war upon it, that the bear people were now his brothers, and that he would never harm another.

These dream people could be anything from the grass eaters, such as the buffalo, deer, or antelope, to the little underwater people, such as the beaver, otter, or muskrat. At other times the dream person might be a bird, but in every case the Indian had to obtain some part of the creature for his medicine.

When the Indians had gone through all these

rituals and preparations, they felt sure that they would have good luck, and, indeed, they usually did.

Upon returning from a good hunt, with enough game so that all in the tribe would have plenty, the Indian hunters always gave thanks to their dream animal, and before feasting they remembered to place a piece of meat in the fire as a thanksgiving offering to the Great Spirit.

The country was large and the game plentiful, yet no tribe could expect to find enough for everyone to eat if they all hunted the same hunting grounds every day. Hunting customs developed, therefore, that protected these grounds.

After the tribes met for their usual spring and fall gatherings, they divided into small groups. The Plains Indians set out in small bands, seeking a campground close to willow trees and rivers. The woodland Indians also had their favorite spots by rivers and lakes. From these camps the bands hunted.

The woodland people, such as the Ojibwa, the Winnebago, and the Menominee, further split up when hunting. Each man, or family, selected his own special hunting territory where no other hunter, unless invited, could set foot. Only in times of famine would these hunting rights be violated. At such times, any man who had the good fortune to bring home game would be welcomed, for the lucky one shared with all in his camp.

Even so, the hunting grounds were not large enough to support the tribes living within their borders. Long ago the Sioux and the Cheyenne Indians lived in what is now Minnesota. As food became harder and harder to get, the Ojibwa, who lived near them, finally made war on the two other tribes, and in time managed to drive them out into the Great Plains. That is the reason we know the Sioux and Cheyenne today as Plains Indians.

Wars between the tribes living near one another were often due to one tribe trespassing on another's hunting grounds. The Blackfeet were forever at war with the Crow, and often the Blackfeet burned the grass on the Crow range. When the wind was right, the fires stampeded the buffalo from the Crow country onto that claimed by the Blackfeet, depriving the Crow of meat.

To indicate the borders of hunting grounds, the Plains Indians marked the area with skulls set on posts or fastened on dead trees. They were either skulls of buffalo or of mountain sheep. Often, however, they were disregarded.

Among the Zuñi Indians in the Southwest, when deer were killed for ceremonial use, they were caught alive and killed by suffocation so that no blood was spilled. Then much honor was given to the spirits of the dead animals.

The bodies were brought into a ceremonial house and placed on the floor. Over them the medicine men draped a ceremonial robe, and around their necks they hung a fine silver and turquoise necklace. Songs, accompanied with rattles, were sung over the dead animals, and then, after scattering corn meal upon them, the meat was finally cooked.

Among those Indians living in permanent villages, such as the Northwest Coast Indians along the Pacific and the Pueblo Indians in the South-

west, other customs developed. On the Pacific Coast the chiefs claimed ownership of the hunting lands. During the beginning of the seasons for fishing, hunting, or berry gathering, the chief called the tribe together and reminded them that the ownership of the land was his. Then he told them that they could now go and use this land. In this way he constantly impressed upon his people that he was a great chief, but also a good and kind man, and the first fruits of these hunts and berry gatherings were brought to him as a gift. After these gifts were collected, the chief and his family then gave a general feast for the entire village. At times, when hunting was good, he invited a neighboring tribe as well.

7

The End of the Trail

Eａｒｌｙ in the eighteenth century, explorers, *voyageurs*, and Jesuit priests braved the unknown wilderness, carrying their explorations through the Great Lakes country and to the headwaters of the Mississippi. The brothers LaVérendrye reached the Black Hills, and Alexander Mackenzie went as far as the Pacific.

Then came the Louisiana Purchase in 1803, followed by the official exploration headed by Meriwether Lewis and William Clark with a small party of only thirty men. The report on their findings, their notes on the wild animals, plants and minerals, the rivers and the mountains, all made a strong impact on the young nation.

At first the mountain men, the trappers, set out. Then John Jacob Astor established his American Fur Company, which offered jobs to adventurous young men as hunters and trappers. Soon other fur companies were started, and they set up posts for trading and built fortifications for protection. Little by little, if the chosen spot was good, the post grew into a settlement, then it became a town, and some, indeed, became great cities.

This exodus of white people began to drive the Indians west. First the Indians were friendly with these new people with much hair on their faces, but as more and more of them came in and the greed of the whites grew, the Indians finally rose up and went on the warpath. Gold was found in the Black Hills, the ancestral land, by then, of the Sioux. This brought on an even larger migration of white people, and within the short span of 100 years the free life of the Indian hunter was ended.

As the open country was settled, the wild animals were also forced west. Many of them died from starvation when forest land was cleared for building towns and for timber. When at last the buffalo had all but been slaughtered, the Indian finally had to give up and accept his fate as a reservation Indian, a ward of the government.

Perhaps the white man thought the land so vast that he could not use it up. In any case, he killed and destroyed whatever stood in his way. He took timbers for building and tall, straight trees for masts on his ships, and never replanted where he cut. Then at last, but almost too late, some men saw the need for saving our wild-life heritage. National parks and national forests were set aside, not only to save the wild life still left within their borders, but also to preserve for future generations the wonders and the beauties of the American wilderness.

With the establishment of these lands, the wild animals gradually returned. Predators, such as wolves, foxes, and coyotes, kept the deer, elk, antelope, and other animals in check, so that in many places these animals did not have the chance to outgrow their natural food supply. Outside the wilderness preserves, the animals also increased in numbers. To keep the wild life within bounds, the various states made hunting laws, setting aside the proper seasons for game to be hunted.

Now the Indian hunter has appeared again. Much of our country is still wild and rugged, and a man not familiar with it can become hopelessly lost. To prevent this and also to be sure of finding game, a hunter will hire an Indian guide. Many white men, born and raised in the wilderness, or close to it, have become guides, but in the north woods of Minnesota, Michigan, and Wisconsin, in Maine and in the provinces of Canada, many of the guides are Indians.

These Indians of today also follow the trap lines of their fathers. They use steel traps, though, and they supply meat to the northern resorts. To this modern hunter the bow and arrow is a weapon of the past; he uses a rifle. Although Indians had to come close to their game with a bow and arrow to be sure of a hit, they are accurate shots with a gun.

94

Some years ago up in Maine a white man stood in conversation with an old Indian when, from back in the woods, a shot rang out. "Hahn!" said the old man. "My boy kills a deer!"

"How do you know he killed it?" asked the visitor.

"He shoots!" was the laconic reply.